Types of Collective Nouns

Collective nouns are varied and numerous, encompassing groups of people, animals, and things. They are specific terms used to describe a collection of individuals or items as a single entity.

The number of collective nouns is not fixed, as new ones can emerge and old ones may fall out of use. The diversity of collective nouns reflects the richness of the English language and its ability to adapt to new contexts and phenomena.

A Troupe of Acrobats

A Coalition of Activists

6

A Cast of Actors

A Fellowship of Adventurers

A Committee of Advisers

A Council of Advisors

A Wing of Airmen

A Coalition of Allies

12

A Coterie of Aristocrats

A Guild of Artisans

14

A Troupe of Artistes

A Group of Artists

A Crew of Astronauts

A Team of Athletes

A Band of Bandits

A Bevy of Beauties

A Congregation of Believers

A Band of Brothers

A Regiment of Cadets

An Entourage of Celebrities

A Cast of Characters

A Team of Cheerleaders

A Brigade of Chefs

A Brood of Children

A Chorus of Choristers

An Assembly of Citizens

A

Sept

of

Clansmen

A Congregation of Clergymen

A Mutiny of Clowns

A Huddle of Coaches

A Gathering of Colleagues

A Panel of Commentators

A Consortium of Companies

A Cabal of Conspirators

A Cluster of Consultants

A Posse of Cowboys

A Syndicate of Criminals

A Panel of Critics

A Bunch of Crooks

A Troupe of Dancers

A Forum of Debaters

A Conference of Delegates

A Deputation of Deputies

A Posse of Detectives

A Delegation of Diplomats

A Board of Directors

A Fleet of Drivers

A Regiment of Drummers

52

A Council of Elders

A Staff of Employees

A Corps of Engineers

A Band of Entertainers

A Club of Enthusiasts

A Suite of Executives

A Panel of Experts

A Horde of Fans

A Crew of Filmmakers

A Brigade of Firefighters

A Fleet of Fishermen

A Entourage of Followers

A Group of Friends

A Cluster of Geniuses

A Cohort of Graduates

A Detachment of Guards

A Party of Guests

A League of Heroes

A Clan of Highlanders

A Podcast of Hosts

A Syndicate of Investors

A Pack of Journalists

A Bench of Judges

An Inquisition of Jurors

A Dynasty of Kings

A Crew of Laborers

A Bevy of Ladies

A Assembly of Lawmakers

A Posse of Lawmen

A Senate of Legislators

An Audience of Listeners

An Illusion of Magicians

A Bench of Magistrates

A Platoon of Marines

A Committee of Members

A Group of Men

A Guild of Merchants

A Council of Ministers

A Court of Monarchs

A Band of Musicians

A Coalition of Nations

A Tribe of Natives

A Caravan of Nomads

A Convent of Nuns

A Regiment of Nurses

A Rank of Officers

A Staff of Officials

A Crowd of Onlookers

A Committee of Organizers

A Congregation of Parishioners

A Host of Participants

A Coalition of Partners

A Gathering of Peers

A Crowd of People

A Troupe of Performers

A Squadron of Pilots

A Team of Players

A Force of Police

A Patrol of Policemen

A Caucus of Politicians

A Ministry of Priests

A Gang of Prisoners

A Network of Professionals

A Faculty of Professors

A Clump of Protesters

A Class of Pupils

A Pack of Rascals

A Band of Rebels

A Family of Relatives

A Delegation of Representatives

A Team of Researchers

A Mob of Rioters

A Band of Roadies

A Gang of Robbers

A Dynasty of Rulers

A Crew of Sailors

A Horde of Savages

A Academy of Scholars

A

Class

of

School Children

A Troop of Scouts

A Staff of Servants

A Colony of Settlers

A Posse of Sheriffs

A Set of Siblings

A Choir of Singers

A Sorority of Sisters

An Battalion of Soldiers

A Panel of Speakers

A Audience of Spectators

A Class of Students

A Crowd of Supporters

A Constellation of Talents

A Faculty of Teachers

A Squad of Teammates

A

Crew

of

Technicians

A Gang of Thieves

A Congregation of Thinkers

A Flock of Tourists

A Caravan of Traders

A Cadre of Trainers

A Caravan of Travelers

A Regiment of Troops

A Board of Trustees

A Set of Twins

A Squad of Volunteers

A Majority of Voters

A Troop of Warriors

A Coven of Witches

A Harem of Wives

A Force of Workers

A Congregation of Worshippers

A Bevy of Writers

www.ingramcontent.com/pod-product-compliance
Lightning Source LLC
Chambersburg PA
CBHW021200100426
42735CB00046B/759

* 9 7 8 1 9 4 9 0 0 2 5 8 4 *